Small Business, Big Success

Kira Ming

DEDICATION

This book is dedicated to God, my mother, and my sister. All three serve different roles, but all three helped make my story of success possible. I want to also dedicate this book to every loyal follower and supporter that has encouraged me along this journey.

Table of Contents

The Beginning

I've always been driven. My mother recently reminded me that at five years old I used to parade around saying how excited I was to go to college. In grade school I was for the most part a straight A student — always on the honor roll, in gifted classes, etc. It was so important for me to focus on getting good grades, because to me, that equaled success. Part of it had to do with the family I came from; full of doctors, lawyers, and educators alike. You were expected to go to school and acquire a good career. That's just the way it went. Anything else was looked down upon. It wasn't until I got older that I realized that yes education was important, but there was so much more to life, success, and wealth.

"It wasn't until I got older that I realized that yes education was important, but there was so much more to life, success, and wealth."

Find Your Why

I've always been an extremely hard worker. I developed my first bit of work ethic from volunteering at the local public library. I created my own schedule, showed up on time, and I loved what I did. I was 14 years old at the time and I had never had so much responsibility. After a while even as a teenager, I started to feel like I should be compensated for my hard work. "Kira, can you put these away?"…"Kira, answer the phone please!"…"Hey Kira can you check out this customer, thanks." But what was I getting from all of this? From a monetary standpoint, nothing — and that bothered me.

"After a while even as a teenager, I started to feel like I should be compensated for my hard work."

Sure, I absolutely loved to read. I was pretty much at the library every day anyway. But it still didn't feel right for me to be working so hard without getting anything in return. After a few months of volunteering there I saw one my of my friends from the community — she had just gotten a job at one of the businesses in the area. "How old do you have to be to get a job there?" I asked. "Just 14," she said. It wasn't long after that I got my first paying job working at the same place. I simply took my work ethic and all of the things I learned volunteering at the library and applied it to a position where I could make money.

"I simply took my work ethic and all of the things I learned volunteering at the library and applied it to a position where I could make money."

My first check started it all. I looked at it...a mere $280 or so — but to a regular 14 year old it was like $1,000. That was the first time I actually felt POWERFUL. I could buy things on my own now. Clothes, a new phone, food. It was at that moment that I made the correlation between hard work and money. I was in paradise until I started wanting more. After a while what I was making was no longer enough. Of course that's when I initially began to realize that I wanted so much more out of life. I was always going to college (I didn't really have a choice because of my family), but now it was time to prepare for that transition.

"I was in paradise until I started wanting more. After a while what I was making was no longer enough."

It was time to make moves so that I could get a good job, and subsequently make more money. Because that's how it goes right? Before I knew it, it was time for me to start applying to colleges. I graduated high school top of my class so I had some pretty good options. My mother wasn't keen on me going too far, and I wasn't keen on going up the street, so I chose an HBCU near the DC area. Campus life was one of the greatest experiences of my life.

"It was time to make moves so that I could get a good job, and subsequently make more money. Because that's how it goes right?"

When it comes to running a successful business you must know the WHY. Without the why you won't get very far. Sure there are plenty of businesses out there that are just money makers, but the most successful business owners and moguls in this world are the ones that passionately believe in their brands and what they have to offer. What's most important is that you're honest with yourself. Do you believe in your business? What's your story? Why are you doing this?

"When it comes to running a successful business you must know the WHY. Without the why you won't get very far."

These are the things that keep you going when being an entrepreneur becomes hard or may even feel impossible. It's the force that drives you; the foundation. It's very important before you move forward to find out the WHY behind starting your business. In discovering your why there are a few questions you can ask yourself. Are you passionate about it? If you don't make money right away will you still do it? What purpose will it serve to the people of this world? These questions can not only serve as a roadmap for you business, but they can also help keep you going when things get tough.

"It's very important before you move forward to find out the WHY behind starting your business."

My mother was always somewhat of a smother mother so I had never really had that much independence before going to college. After beginning college for the first time I felt like a grownup. I was fortunate enough to have gotten work-study freshman year. My checks ended up being around the same amount as the ones from my first job. All I kept thinking was, "Hang in there, this won't be forever." It became a depressing cycle. I would work my behind off while going to school, get paid pennies, and be broke within a few hours. This went on for years. Needless to say, I just kept thinking there had to be a better way.

"I would work my behind off while going to school, get paid pennies, and be broke within a few hours. This went on for years. Needless to say, I just kept thinking there had to be a better way."

I had a lot of inspiration. I come from a very musically inclined family. Many of my cousins play instruments, my sister and I both sing. Music was always a major part of my upbringing and who I was. I grew up listening to a lot of rock. Classic rock, folk rock — you name it. We also listened to a lot of Latin music in my house…bachata, merengue, salsa. My sister always did her own thing so she listened to Hip Hop, and that's really the only time I was exposed to it. Not too long before starting college I came across some old classic Hip Hop songs. I was so little when they came out that I never placed the songs with the artists. I fell in love. I started going back in time, re-discovering every classic Hip Hop album there was; that led to me discovering pretty much every artist from that era…The Golden Age of Hip Hop. That's what I became obsessed with.

"I started going back in time, re-discovering every classic Hip Hop album there was; that led to me discovering pretty much every artist from that era…The Golden Age of Hip Hop."

The Creation

By this point I had changed my major from pre-med to psychology. The more I delved into music, the more I realized how passionate I was about it. I remember picking up an autobiography of one of the most successful writers in Hip Hop and saying, "This is it, this is what I want to do." It was junior year (at this point my final major was English), and the only thing I knew was that I loved writing and I loved music. So how do you combine the two? What would you call it? You'd call it entertainment journalism. I immediately started to do research on jobs that fit the bill. I got offered to move forward with internships from two major Hip Hop publications in New York, but there was one problem — they were both in New York City. I just couldn't pick up and leave. At this point I was becoming discouraged. I had finally found what I wanted to do…and I couldn't do it because of circumstances.

"The more I delved into music, the more I realized how passionate I was about it."

And then it hit me like a brick - WHY NOT START YOUR OWN? I was a naturally amazing writer, and by this time I knew the Hip Hop genre inside and out, and I had a lot to talk about. I signed onto a free blog platform…and started a blog. My first entry was on one of my favorite artists of all time. It was just a few paragraphs and an image of them placed on the side. I was proud. I looked at the "complete" page and said this is mine. I created this. It was at that moment that I realized IF THERE ISN'T AN OPPORTUNITY, CREATE ONE. I started to share it with others and was surprised by all of the love it got! People really supported it, even if at the moment I didn't quite realize what I had. It received so much support that I started thinking why not make it bigger — why not make it a publication.

"It was at that moment that I realized IF THERE ISN'T AN OPPORTUNITY, CREATE ONE."

Of course, if I was going to make something print, it couldn't just be a blog. It would need to be…a magazine. After going back and forth on names — trying to think of something unique — something that stood out from all of the other names I'd heard, I came up with a one of a kind name for my business. I had no clue what I was doing. No clue how to run a magazine. I just knew I had to make it happen, somehow. I started looking through all of the magazines that I'd read. What was the format? What was the content? I knew I had a long road ahead of me but I was ready.

"No clue how to run a magazine. I just knew I had to make it happen, somehow."

I knew that if it was going to be successful, it would take a lot of research and a lot of work. First I would need to learn about publishing in general. Between my background in library science, my involvement in the University newspaper, and majoring in English, I knew a tad about editorial and publishing, but that would only cover the basics. First I would have to decide whether this would be a traditional print magazine, or a digital one. If I went print, would I have to land a distribution deal or shop it around to willing vendors? Was going the print route even worth it?

"I knew that if it was going to be successful, it would take a lot of research and a lot of work."

Even after I figured some of these things out there were more questions. What kinds of articles would it have? Who would be my readers? I began to feel overwhelmed...and then I started to remember my strong-point. Organization. Since a little girl, I have always been the most organized person I knew — even more than adults, sometimes. I realized that organization would be my best friend. I started writing articles, summarizing the artists' background, track record, and what they work working on. This helped everything start to make sense.

"I began to feel overwhelmed...and then I started to remember my strong-point. Organization."

Then I thought, wouldn't it be that much better if I could sit down and speak with these artists directly? So I started to compile a list of everyone that I wanted to interview. I knew I wouldn't be able to interview all of them (yet), but it was important to make the list anyway. I also knew that it was time to have an official website. At this point I didn't even know the difference between a domain name and a host site. After searching far and wide, I finally settled on a website that offered domain purchasing and an internal web designer. I was sold. This was the beginning.

"After searching far and wide, I finally settled on a website that offered domain purchasing and an internal web designer. I was sold."

I had more questions. Do people even pick up a book or a magazine any more? The answer wasn't so cut and dry. For me, I'm old school, so I valued the printing process, and for me, nothing replaces the experience of turning each page of a publication. Though this was my sentiment, I had to consider reality — we live in a digital age. Everything is online. So I figured why not do both? It was at that moment that I settled on a digital platform, with a printing option being the end goal. Although digital would be the main outlet, I still needed to be well versed on magazine specifics. Over time I began to immerse myself in learning about magazine layout including printing service options, printing dimensions, font sizing, image licensing, glossy vs matte, columns, etc. At this point I felt like I had a strong sense of what I wanted the end result to be. The process of getting the actual website built was a tedious one.

"Though this was my sentiment, I had to consider reality — we live in a digital age."

As far as the website, obviously, I could have paid someone to design it, but the goal was to make money not spend it right? I ended up using the site's internal web builder to create a basic layout. I was smart enough to know that no one would take me seriously if I didn't have an official domain name. This is where I learned that you have to spend money to make money. Creating a functioning website was free, owning your domain name wasn't. I reluctantly purchased my domain name and then it was even more official. So at this point my website is complete, I had an associated email address, and I found someone to design my first logo. *crickets*...now what?

"I was smart enough to know that no one would take me seriously if I didn't have an official domain name."

I wasn't quite sure how I was going to make this successful but I knew I would. For the high traffic piece I had to learn quite a bit. First I had to learn that people wouldn't just show up to your site. You had to actually DRIVE traffic. I learned that your website shouldn't have many layers in the beginning; make it as clean and simple as possible. This really does play a role in how you're placed in search engines, etc. Little by little I gained knowledge about keywords, SEO, and backlinks. As far as the artist part believe it or not that came easy. I had a system for how I acquired interviews, and I ended up interviewing a great deal of people. People that individuals doing this for decades hadn't been able to land. Each celeb that I interviewed gave me even more respect and notoriety in the industry.

"First I had to learn that people wouldn't just show up to your site. You had to actually DRIVE traffic."

We will learn later how those old interviews worked for me even years later. At this point the question still remained, do I go print? The internet is taking over more and more and quite frankly, I never see anyone with a book in their hand these days. I wondered if it was worth the effort. I knew that the road to reach success with my business would entail a lot of everything. A lot of marketing, a lot of networking, and a lot of strategizing. My plan was simple. Place ads and promote online, get out and host, collaborate with other businesses, network at events offline, and try to automate as much as possible to reach my goals.

"The internet is taking over more and more and quite frankly, I never see anyone with a book in their hand these days."

The Legal Basics

I didn't know much about running a business but I knew there would be some legal steps to take so that everything would be solid. Many people are familiar with the terminology associated with establishing a business, but few have an understanding of exactly what these terms mean, and their purpose. Most of the legal steps you need to take can be done without a lawyer, but always do your research and use the resources that make you feel most comfortable. It would take me some time to cover everything, but if I followed the guidelines and had great bookkeeping and organization, I could set everything up and protect my brand without shelling out any unnecessary money. I knew the magazine was one of kind, which made it even more important to take everything concerning it seriously.

"Most of the legal steps you need to take can be done without a lawyer, but always do your research and use the resources that make you feel most comfortable."

Trademark and Copyright - You invite your friends over for a brainstorming party, you search for synonyms online, you squint your eyes real hard to come up with a name and VOILA! You've found the perfect name for your business. You create your website, get pens and pencils made, business cards and coffee mugs. Seek legal counsel and make sure everything is tied to you with the right protection. Often the name of your business is a direct reflection of you and what you do, so if you have things to prove it was yours first a lawyer may be able to help you if anything unfortunate happens — but if you can save the headache, do so.

"Seek legal counsel and make sure everything is tied to you with the right protection."

In another example, you've spent weeks choosing the colors you want to represent your brand. You've gone through a ton of symbols, drawings, etc. and now you have the perfect logo. Protect it! Generally, logos are less in danger of being stolen because they're so detailed, and often reflect the business name, yet in still, protect your official logo, even if you think you'll change it down the line. Someone I knew who happened to be an amazing artist, designed my first logo. It was a simple orange spray can, spraying orange paint. Of course the logo would evolve over the years, and that's ok...until it's time to change it, protect it as much as you can and retain source files — your proof.

"You've gone through a ton of symbols, drawings, etc. and now you have the perfect logo. Protect it!"

Register -You want to be right within your state (if applicable) as well as on the federal level. The purpose of registering your business is to let the government know that there is in fact a business and second, so that you can be taxed appropriately. For these reasons and more, you want to register your business properly. The type of license depends on the business. A brick-and-mortar establishment may require a different license or registration than an online business. An online magazine may require a different license than an online store. Do as much research as possible to find out exactly what licenses you need to have or steps you need to take to legally operate your business and be in compliance with state and federal regulations. Not every type of business will require the same paperwork.

"A brick-and-mortar establishment may require a different license or registration than an online business."

Supply And Demand: Who's Buying

Once I got the basics down I thought I was good to go. But of course, there was more. Seeing as though this was a magazine, I knew I would have to actually...print something. I started researching printing companies. How much per page, what font would I use, how many pages would it be, would it be glossy or matte finish were some of the questions that arose. After going through all of these things in my mind I started talking to people. I shared what the plan was for the magazine. They loved it, but only the website part. Many people believed that society just didn't read anymore.

"I shared what the plan was for the magazine. They loved it, but only the website part. Many people believed that society just didn't read anymore."

Up until that point I hadn't thought about supply and demand. I hadn't thought about who would actually read the magazine, and if there was in fact a need for it. I mean obviously people read, but what are they reading, and why? In addition, how were they reading it? I realized that the need was authenticity. Was I passionate about the music I supported and the people that were considered legends? Absolutely. But what did that have to do with running a business? Nothing. I happened to come up with this idea during a time where many "Hip Hop Heads" were getting fed up with what was being played on the radio. They felt like mainstream music was going in a bad direction, and they were looking to old school music and underground artists for solace.

"They felt like mainstream music was going in a bad direction, and they were looking to old school music and underground artists for solace."

There was a need. I knew right away my publication was something special. My readers needed an outlet, and I was it. Not only did I ignite excitement from going back in time and honoring musical legends, but I ignited excitement among the new up and coming artists who had real talent but felt like they didn't have a platform. My brand was more important than I could ever imagine. Every radio station, magazine, and tv outlet had the same content, and highlighted the same people. Mine would do something different. That's when I realized there was in fact a place for my business in the market, and a demand.

"Every radio station, magazine, and TV outlet had the same content, and highlighted the same people. Mine would do something different."

We get so passionate about our businesses that we are offended by the thought that our businesses are anything but necessary. That's not always the case. Need versus want. Does your business supply a need or want? Does it solve a problem? If you sell bottled water chances are people will in fact purchase from you. Water is one of the most important substances known to mankind. Now, if you sell a beautiful nail polish — I know you don't want to hear it, but many don't consider that a need. What does this mean? It means you need to tailor your sales approach to your business. If you know nail polish isn't often considered a need, your job is to convince people why they need to have this amazing polish in their lives. You need to convert want to need. It's the holidays, you NEED to purchase this nail polish for your wife. You keep wasting money going back to the salon because of chipped paint, you NEED this non-crack polish. And there you are, a solution to a problem.

"We get so passionate about our businesses that we are offended by the thought that our businesses are anything but necessary."

In order for your business to be successful there has to be a need for what you're offering. Your business should be a solution to a problem. Sure, you may adore your singing candles that glow in the dark, but is there a market for it? Do people need it? And if they don't, can you convince them that they do? This also ties into marketing, but we'll discuss that later. Do research. Find out what consumers are purchasing. Of course you want to be an innovator, and stand out in the market, but it should still be something that people will actually purchase. If your business happens to be something that people aren't checking for, be creative and find ways to market it so that it sells. Are the chances of people beating down the door for your singing candles high? Not really. But how about including them in themed gift bags? Or hosting candle making parties? I can't say this enough, GET CREATIVE. There is nothing people won't buy if they're convinced right.

"I can't say this enough, GET CREATIVE. There is nothing people won't buy if they're convinced right."

There are numerous ways to conduct research and get feedback on the market and see what's selling. For one, you can hit the pavement and get out in the fields to ask people about what they're buying. Of course these days you can easily do research via the web as well. Research things like how much your industry is grossing annually, who is buying what, and who is at the top of the market for what you sell. More specifically, you can do surveys, polls, and focus groups to get more personal and detailed feedback. Let this information mold how you package and present your business to the world. If you find that there isn't a high demand for what you do don't worry; sometimes you have to TELL people what they want. It may be difficult, but once you do you've cracked the code.

"If you find that there isn't a high demand for what you do don't worry; sometimes you have to TELL people what they want."

Map It Out: What's Your Plan

At this point I had birthed my business baby. I had the gift, then I developed the idea, then I got to work and began building the business. But now what? Clearly I had never run a business and especially not a publication before. So what was the game plan? As I mentioned before I realized the key would be getting and staying organized. I created an email account, and within that created subfolders that I felt would help me categorize correspondence. So now, I have an email account where I can organize and file away all of the emails pertinent to running my business. But what about everything else? I would need some way to file things, and a place to hold and store things. I decided on an electronic notebook app.

"I would need some way to file things, and a place to hold and store things. I decided on an electronic notebook app."

This tool would be my best friend in years to come. You could create notebooks, and within notebooks you could create notes. But these weren't just notes. They could be mini files, or at least lead you to your files. My notebooks were filled with outlines, checklists, account info, write ups and more. It made mapping out my business literally as easy as clicking a button. So now what were my goals? What I've realized in running a business is that if you don't have goals, solid goals...you'll end up going in circles. I knew early on that my goals were to get a high volume of traffic to my website, interview as many notable artists as possible, and eventually go print.

"What I've realized in running a business is that if you don't have goals, solid goals...you'll end up going in circles."

Unless you have a super brain you will need a plan. What do you want to accomplish? What are your short term goals? Long term goals? What do you want to experience? You need to map everything out according to where you are, and where you want to go. Where do you see yourself? Where do you want to be? How much money do you want to make, or is success to you denoted by something else? These questions are important, and will ultimately determine the success of your business.

"These questions are important, and will ultimately determine the success of your business."

The Importance of A Website

I cannot stress the importance of having a website enough. In my opinion, no matter what kind of business you have the website serves as an anchor. It is the "home" or the "base" of your business. There are all kinds of websites and they vary, but a good website can serve many purposes. On a website, the homepage or landing page typically serves as your business in a nutshell. The title, logo, and anything else defining your company should be the first thing that people they see when they visit. Good homepages usually indicate a little bit about the company as well. They typically highlight any special promotion or happenings, and they should attract the attention of the visitor immediately.

"In my opinion, no matter what kind of business you have the website serves as an anchor."

Studies show that the average user spends a great deal of their time looking at the left-hand side of a website, and at the information that appears at the top — the information not requiring scrolling. This gives you minimal time to capture people's' attention. The remainder of the site should be filled with appropriate content for your business. You want to make sure you include background information on the website as well for people who come there just for that. The website also serves as a tool for contact. All websites should have your company's contact information so that people can reach you to do business. All in all your website is like your business' home. Consumers and patrons these days are lazy. They don't want to work too hard, so it's important to have a space where customers have everything they need in one place.

"They don't want to work too hard, so it's important to have a space where customers have everything they need in one place."

Don't Do It Alone: Join Forces

Once you really start running your business things can be overwhelming. This means you may need help. When you have a good product or service, this will come naturally. As I started to make progress, other companies wanted to collaborate with me. Various companies wanted to put on showcases, open mics, and industry nights. Every type of event you can think of. I had to learn about securing a venue, presale tickets versus pay at the door, bar service, schedule of events, and so much more.

"Once you really start running your business things can be overwhelming. This means you may need help."

A good journalist is always prepared. Then it's the interview itself. For the longest time I wanted to keep all articles print. This meant that when I interviewed someone in person or via phone the interview would have to be transcribed — converted from audio to print. This process could take hours...and it usually did. Then it's implementation time. Creating the online issue. Yet another long drawn out process preceding a feature being published and going live. After all is said and done, you still have to promote and market the new feature. This can entail promo schedules, etc. In other words, there is A LOT that goes into featuring an artist and giving an artist the exposure they desire using your resources. I would definitely need to work with others from time to time.

"In other words, there is A LOT that goes into featuring an artist and giving an artist the exposure they desire using your resources."

Working with others can be tricky, trust me I know. There is definitely an art to it. Everyone approaches it differently but there are dos and don'ts and ways to avoid disaster. I find that the best collabs occur naturally; meaning two matches made in heaven that end up coming together in a way that makes sense. If you're a shoe company you may not partner with a doggie biscuit company...but don't speak too soon. That doesn't mean that a shoe company can't come together with a cupcake company. How in the world would that work out you ask? Imagine a showing of your new spring line; showcasing the newest shoe designs, sponsored by the cupcake company. Guests are welcomed to a wonderful variety of cupcakes while they view the new shoes, network, and place their preorders.

"I find that the best collabs occur naturally; meaning two matches made in heaven that end up coming together in a way that makes sense."

You definitely want it to make sense. Before collaborating with anyone, sit down and ask yourselves will this work. How can we come together in a productive way that will benefit both parties? If you find it's a good combo then move forward with a contract. Not having a contract or at least some type of write up or outline is a disaster waiting to happen. Everyone's agreement will be different, but I would think everyone's contract would include what the event or collaboration will entail. Who is providing what, event details, who will gain on the backend (i.e. who will make the profit from the collab; will it be split, etc.), what both of your responsibilities are, and how both of you will be promoted in the endeavor. Again, always seek legal counsel as applicable.

"Not having a contract or at least some type of write up or outline is a disaster waiting to happen."

Using the shoe/cupcake example, perhaps the cupcake is listed on the promotional flyer as a sponsor. They provide the cupcakes, and they get 5% of each sale made that day from preorders. The result of a successful collaboration can be major. You can make money directly from an event or campaign, you can save money with overhead costs (i.e. you host it in the cupcake company's lounge), you've now reached their following, and word of mouth is often after you've left a good taste in another company's mouth. Typically when you have a successful collab businesses want to work with you over and over again and you got it, it continues to be beneficial if done right.

"Typically when you have a successful collab businesses want to work with you over and over again."

Building A Strong Team

I have always been an independent person. I'm a firm believer in if you want something done right, do it yourself. I just don't like asking people for help and even past that I just know how I want things done — in my mind no one can carry out that vision for me. Though that may true for many, you still need help. God has given everyone different gifts in this life, but there are people that have gifts that you don't have. Those are the people who you should use. I learned early on that you will need people to bring things together and carry out your vision. When I first started building my brand I realized how much I needed. For example, I needed professional photos, and I was no photographer — so I would need one.

"I just don't like asking people for help and even past that I just know how I want things done — in my mind no one can carry out that vision for me."

I was fortunate because someone very close to me linked me with a local photographer who was more than happy to be part of what I was building. With him I did my first photoshoot. As mentioned before, my first logo was developed by someone else as well, something I couldn't do either. I was blessed because in my case my photography and graphic/visual needs were really the only areas where I needed others to help. That was until the brand began to grow bigger and bigger, and it became overwhelming for me to even write at times. It became less about me writing, interviewing, and reviewing and more about me running the business. So I had to find some writers. I was just starting out so finding a writer and paying them a large amount of money was out. I knew where my brand was going, and that eventually after all of the hard work there would be a lot of exposure for anyone who was associated with the brand.

"It became less about me writing, interviewing, and reviewing and more about me running the business"

Now that you know the reason everyone needs good people on their team, there are ways to make sure you get just that. If you are just starting out, perhaps you don't have a big salary to reel them in. But if you have a good brand, and you are creative you can build a solid team. One way is to offer an internship. The down part about this is that internships are short term, usually between 3 and 6 months. Then you have to find another intern. The good part is that if you establish a good system of recruiting interns on an ongoing basis, you'll never have a lapse in help, and typically it is for their school credit. Another way to attract team members is to sell them on the experience or exposure. If a photographer believes in your brand and where it's going, they may not mind taking a few promo shoots for the credit and to add to their professional portfolio.

"But if you have a good brand, and you are creative you can build a solid team."

How Do I Make Money?

By this point I could honestly say I knew how to run a business, and that the business actually had a place in the world. After many years of successful interviews, having successful events, and getting people to believe in my brand, I realized something. I wasn't making any money. I had learned so much, and worked so hard to build the brand that I forgot about what to me is the most important thing after passion, and that is making money.

"I had learned so much, and worked so hard to build the brand that I forgot about what to me is the most important thing after passion, and that is making money."

So I went back to the drawing board and started to think about how I could monetize my business. If it's one thing that I've learned it's that your business should solve a problem. I knew I was a skilled writer, and by this time I knew I had a loyal following and a lot of impressive things under my belt...but what problem was I solving? One of things I noticed from the magazine's inception was that a lot of underground, unsigned, and indie artists wanted to be featured, even if they weren't solicited. Many artists were frustrated that they didn't have a platform to be highlighted, and that they couldn't reach a greater amount of people. They also needed a great deal of promotion, marketing, and press. So there it was. The problem was that unsigned artists needed a platform, promotion, and branding and the solution was that my publication could provide that in depth.

"Many artists were frustrated that they didn't have a platform to be highlighted, and that they couldn't reach a greater amount of people."

Even with this eureka moment I still wasn't immediately generating revenue. What was I doing wrong? Spreading the word about good music was my passion. When thinking about what to offer artists I had to consider a few things. Number one, some of the artists who solicited features or promotion weren't always my personal taste. But they still wanted a shot to reach people and market their projects. I thought about how if they hired a manager, they'd have to pay that manager a fee, when they got promotional material made they would have to pay for that merchandise, and when they recorded, they would have to pay the studio. So, it made sense to offer service options for things that would help advance their careers.

"I thought about how if they hired a manager, they'd have to pay that manager a fee, when they got promotional material made they would have to pay for that merchandise, and when they recorded, they would have to pay the studio."

I figured, let artists register to be featured, promote them to everyone within my large network for maximum exposure, and let THE PEOPLE decide if they're feeling the music or not. That way everyone gets a chance to shine, and a chance to prove themselves without my biased feature selection. It only made sense. When it came to featuring an artist, there were so many components. You had to first do your research. Although these artists were often not considered "well knowns" as of yet, they still had a background that I needed to be familiar with. They had a story. They had social media presence (that would grow as a result of working with me), and of course they had music.

"They had social media presence (that would grow as a result of working with me), and of course they had music."

Now that I had a solid model for how the magazine would generate revenue, it was time to maximize profit by creating effective marketing tactics. In a day and age that's almost completely internet driven, I felt like I needed to give the most attention to social media marketing. What were the most popular social media sites? Which ones pertained to my business? What would I need to post to reach the most people in the most effective way?

"In a day and age that's almost completely internet driven, I felt like I needed to give the most attention to social media marketing."

So you're doing everything right. You have an efficient website, you're using free marketing tools to your advantage, you're working with people left and right, and you do everything in your power to make sure your company has integrity. But still, no sales. Have you ever went to the mall, been attracted to a kiosk, saw something you liked that you knew that was a good product, and still didn't buy it? Same thing. The key to converting leads to sales is thinking like a consumer. What do you typically look for when you purchase something or use a service? Number one you have to get real about your business.

"The key to converting leads to sales is thinking like a consumer."

Let's rewind for a moment. If you have an innovative business idea, a solid foundation, and an efficient marketing plan, you should expect results. But are you prepared for them? If your goal is to make money, think about how you will receive and handle that money. A few questions you should ask yourself should be how will customers submit payment? Will you have a business account and a business line of credit, or will everything be tied to you as an individual service provider? Today, it is easier than ever to invoice, receive payments, and bookkeep all in one central place. Do your research and decide what works for you.

"If you have an innovative business idea, a solid foundation, and an efficient marketing plan, you should expect results."

Pricing - Pricing your product or services can get tricky. There is a balance between researching industry standards and pricing competitively. It all depends on your brand (which as it relates to this has nothing to do with packaging). If you have a product that you feel is high quality, and it takes a great deal of money to produce, you may want to keep your pricing at an industry standard, or maybe even higher — to reflect that your product is a premier product. If you have a product or service that is a bit more common, you may want your advantage to be a good product at a low price. Both types of pricing have a consumer base. People will pay high for a good, high quality product but people will always appreciate a bargain. A good way to benefit from both pricing models is to have standard pricing, but offer discounts or promotional pricing.

"People will pay high for a good, high quality product but people will always appreciate a bargain."

There was this important little sector that I would need to master. Marketing. How would I bring people to my site, and once I did, then what? In the day and age of social media I realized that internet marketing would be my best friend. It was free, fast, and reached large amounts of people. I quickly set up fan pages, company pages, and "groups" to help give the magazine an online presence. Over time, this would have a major effect on the growth of the magazine. Not only did I use social media as a tool to spread the word, it also served as inspiration. So many people were excited about what my publication represented. A few followers turned to thousands. Sounds like success right? Not quite. As we've discussed, there must be a method to driving business.

"Not only did I use social media as a tool to spread the word, it also served as inspiration."

Sales conversion is one of the most important skills you will learn while running a business. Oddly enough it's generally the hardest. The great part is once you learn the art of conversion and generating multiple streams of income chances are you've made it. So in my case how does a magazine make money? Good question. First, you have the magazine itself. Bottom line, a good publication will generate purchasing readers. You are a creator of a product that people want.

"The great part is once you learn the art of conversion and generating multiple streams of income chances are you've made it."

The goal is to get people to purchase. Each unit moved will yield a profit. Thanks to innovation there are now companies that will print, package, and ship your publication for you for a small fee. Next I took a look at the website. How do websites within themselves make money? The answer is mostly through ads. Various programs allow you to make money from your website by allowing them to strategically place relative ads on your site in return for payment. In essence, the more traffic you bring to your site the more money you make.

"In essence, the more traffic you bring to your site the more money you make."

Use Platforms To Your Advantage

Once I got clear on all of these concepts, it was easy to develop a social media marketing plan. Auto-schedulers are social media marketing tools that allow you to schedule your posts in advance — so that even when you're sleeping, your business is still marketing itself. It was genius. It made life so much easier. My routine was to project what I needed to promote or market for the upcoming week, this would include the month's feature, any special events coming up, or any special promotions. Then I would schedule the posts for the entire upcoming week. I would still post and promote manually (because you don't want to become impersonal and engagement is imperative), but that would be additional promotion on top of an already solid marketing schedule.

"Auto-schedulers are social media marketing tools that allow you to schedule your posts in advance — so that even when you're sleeping, your business is still marketing itself."

The next tactic would be something that I had been doing already in great number, events. As we discovered earlier, collaboration is key. If I came across a record label I would feature their artists in return for a joint showcase event. If a non-profit had certain initiatives that tied into what I was doing I would work with them to give back whether it be with knowledge, fundraising, or resources. Holding or attending events is probably one of the most essential marketing strategies you can use. It's an up close and personal way to sell your product or service as well as yourself. It shows that you know what you're doing, you know the industry, and you're confident enough to show up as an expert in your field.

"It shows that you know what you're doing, you know the industry, and you're confident enough to show up as an expert in your field."

After a few years I had the opportunity to become a radio host, and of course I used that as a platform to spread the word about my brand as well. The director was gracious enough to give me a segment on the station's weekly Hip Hop show. I was starting to gain a name for myself as owner of the magazine, which was very different for me because I had gotten so comfortable being behind the scenes. I loved running my business and being the brains behind such a dope movement. Now people wanted to see who was behind the brand, and that was scary.

"I was starting to gain a name for myself as owner of the magazine, which was very different for me because I had gotten so comfortable being behind the scenes."

The use of platforms is essential in marketing to increase your reach and drive revenue. Let me further explain how using platforms can grow your business. So you've created a business. Your business is outlined, mapped out, and everything pertaining to it is solid. You just do what you do, and you stay in your lane. Say you have a natural hair care line with a variety of products. Your business is doing well, you have regular customers that only use natural products, and they of course want your products. Here and there they refer you to other women who also use natural products.

"The use of platforms is essential in marketing to increase your reach and drive revenue."

But now what? Sure, as you market and promote you'll reach all of the natural ladies out there, and hopefully sell to them. And hopefully they'll be returning customers, and in return hopefully they'll continue to tell others. But eventually you will reach a plateau...why you say? Because you aren't reaching other customers — new customers. You aren't pulling people to your products — you are preaching to the choir. And that stunts growth.

"You aren't pulling people to your products — you are preaching to the choir. And that stunts growth."

Now, when it comes time to utilize the art of platforms there is a right way to do things. Say you meet a radio show host that has a show about beauty. Makeup, hair, fashion...now you aren't a radio personality. You don't even like talking. Why in the world would you go on the radio? An example — you go on the show and the topic of the week is how perms can cause permanent damage to your hair. You weigh in on this and inform the listeners about how it destroys follicles, and leaves you with no edges in the end. Blowdrying your hair out is a safer, more natural alternative...as long as you protect your hair.

"Now, when it comes time to utilize the art of platforms there is a right way to do things."

Your business offers a heat protectant of course. At the end of the show you are thanked and asked to tell people where they can check you out and purchase your products — mind you the radio show reaches 1,000 listeners. 500 of them use perms, and 100 of them will no longer be doing so. They want a "blow out," and thus place an order for your heat protectant, with a special discount applied from listening in to the show — but they can't leave without your hot oil, and natural edge smoother. All together a value of $100.

"At the end of the show you are thanked and asked to tell people where they can check you out and purchase your products — mind you the radio show reaches 1,000 listeners. 500 of them use perms, and 100 of them will no longer be doing so."

That is $1000 you've made from a 1 hour show, by simply talking about a relevant topic, and plugging your business. Why in the world wouldn't you want to make $1,000 from 1 hour of your time a week? That's $4,000 extra a month, and $48,000 annually. Again, just from 1 hour on a radio show. It makes no sense not to use other platforms to your advantage — to see more of those dollars and expand your reach and brand visibility both online and offline.

"It makes no sense not to use other platforms to your advantage — to see more of those dollars and expand your reach and brand visibility both online and offline."

Your Marketing Message

Engagement - We've talked about how to become clear on what you do and where it belongs in the world. We've also covered how to automate and simplify many of the marketing tasks that all businesses need to tackle. But there is another important element — engagement. A common mistake many businesses make is not having enough of it. The notion is that if there is a quality product or service, and you work hard to put the product or services out there, that nothing else needs to be done. Sure, those who want what you have to offer will purchase from you. But others need to be convinced. They need to feel like they know you. Believe it or not, getting personal with your potential customers is a great way to not only drive sales, but keep consumers coming back for more. They know you. They know your brand. They feel more involved in promoting something great. Everyone engages their audience differently, but many common forms of social media engagement are asking questions, posting quotes, or sharing relative memes or images that in return yield response.

"But there is another important element — engagement."

Social Media Marketing: There Is An Art

Internet and social media marketing can only do but so much. Yes you reach a large amount of people, but those people aren't going to necessarily be your customers. You want to zero in on your target market. Who is your ideal customer? How old are they? Where do they live? What are their interests? These things are important so that you can make sure you're targeting the right people.

"These things are important so that you can make sure you're targeting the right people."

Once you become clear on that, it's time to get creative with your marketing. You cannot simply post advertisements all day and expect to reach your fullest potential! You must get creative. Perhaps have a different theme each day of the week. Not only does this show that you're consistent, it gets people looking forward to topics that interest them each week. When it comes to social media, visual marketing is key. Images are statistically known to capture the attention of your audience more than just words. Another great way to use social media to grow your brand is by creating videos and doing livestreams. There is no cut and dry way to market using social media. Do what works for you, but be consistent. It is free!

"You cannot simply post advertisements all day and expect to reach your fullest potential!"

Offline Marketing: The Web Isn't Enough

As I mentioned earlier, events are a great way to promote your business. Whether you attend them or host them, you will reach people. When you attend an event you are most likely meeting people with like minds, or people who are interested in what you're selling. This is where those good old people skills come in handy. Talk to people, pass out business cards — connect. You are your brand's biggest ambassador! Nine times out of ten these people don't know you or your company so it's important to introduce yourself and your brand with confidence.

"When you attend an event you are most likely meeting people with like minds, or people who are interested in what you're selling."

Collaborating and cross promoting are so important! I cannot stress the importance of this enough. When it came to the magazine, I started alone. Not long after I would connect with others in the industry. They wanted to work together. With me just starting out and no revenue, I wondered how I could possibly be of any benefit to them. Then it hit me. I have something they want....they have something I want. A collaboration or trade off would benefit both parties. Perhaps they would throw an event, and I would cover it. In return, they would mention my magazine as a sponsor — this often included my logo on promotional material. I paid nothing — but what did I gain? Exposure, more potential readers, free advertisement, and notoriety. I had successfully learned the art of using what you have to gain momentum, even when you don't have a large budget. And this was a great way to get offline.

"I had successfully learned the art of using what you have to gain momentum, even when you don't have a large budget."

Be Creative: Think Outside The Box

One of the most important things you can do as a business owner is to remain creative. When you work for someone else, you essentially show up to work, do your job, and get paid. When you are running a business, the fate of the business is in your hands. No one can put a spin on what you do better than you. Connect with people you've never connected with before, try different marketing approaches, pull in a different group of people. The possibilities are endless, and you will need to explore as many of them as possible to stand out in an already competitive world.

"No one can put a spin on what you do better than you."

Be Clear On Your Offers

Developing your business offers can be a difficult task although it may sound easy. The misconception is that if you have a product then specifying your offers should come easily, unlike with services. This isn't true. Even if you have products, you must still have enticing offers. Perhaps if you have a skin care line you may have a dry skin collection of items that can be purchased a la carte or within a bundle. Perhaps a special bonus item is included with bundle purchases. Of course if you have a life coaching business it may be a tad easier to create offers. Many common offers in this area include classes, bootcamps, or one-on-one coaching for example. Take time to truly assess what you offer, and how you want to offer it to consumers. Keep your goals in mind while doing this.

"The misconception is that if you have a product then specifying your offers should come easily, unlike with services."

71

Everyone Loves A Sale: Promotions And Sales Work

It doesn't matter what industry you're in, sales and promotions are a must! Even the most serious, cut and dry businesses need this element to some extent. You'd be surprised how your brain starts ticking with ideas once you open up. Own a pet grooming business? Have a pet spa day where you offer discounts to those people who want pretty pets! Sell cupcakes? Have a mother daughter tea, featuring your cupcakes. Great way to promote your business and earn revenue! Don't put yourself in a box of this is what I do, so this is all I can do.

"Don't put yourself in a box of this is what I do, so this is all I can do."

Why Is Branding Important?

Branding and Packaging - This is important. Branding is everything! It's how people recognize your company. It's the face of your business. Branding is far more than what you think. Sure, elements of branding include logos, slogans, etc. But in essence it's more about who your company is to the core. It's about what your company represents and what customers expect from your business. A standard. If you have a transportation service and your motto is "always on time" but 90% of your pickups are late, you can have all of the cool logos you want, you don't have a reputable brand! Make sure you put as much emphasis on the integrity of your company as you do packaging. Of course a few cool pens wouldn't hurt.

"It's about what your company represents and what customers expect from your business."

You Are Your Biggest Ambassador

After many years of growing my brand it was time for me to come out of my shell. I come from a family of strong and outgoing personalities. My mother is outgoing, my sister is outgoing. I am not. I am actually very shy unless I know you, or have had some spirits. But after doing the radio show for awhile, I had no choice. I had to be on air each and every week and sell my love for Hip Hop. I had to promote and MAKE people pay attention to what we were saying. I had to make artists BUY into what opportunities we created for them. These things would be a major game changer for how I ran my business. I took all of those things I had to do for the radio show and applied them to running the magazine.

"I had to promote and MAKE people pay attention to what we were saying."

After many years of hiding, it was time. My mother would go out and people would tell her they had heard of my magazine — legends and people in very high places within the industry were reaching out to keep up with what I was doing. I had a solid, yet growing company. It was my brand. When people heard my publication's name they immediately knew what it represented. Everyone was doing entertainment coverage of some sort — blogs, vlogs, articles, magazines...but no one was honoring true Hip Hop culture. No one was covering unsigned talent and the greats that may have been forgotten even though they're legends. That's what my publication did. The more visible I became the more I started to influence others.

"When people heard my publication's name they immediately knew what it represented."

So many people began to admire how I did business, the hustle spirit I was starting to develop, and the grind I was on. People wanted to know how I gained followers, how I ran the website, how I marketed so often while still working a 9-5. I never really had an answer for them. I just knew I did what was necessary to run my business. The more questions I received the more I realized I had so much to offer to others. People were inspired. They wanted to know how to be successful in business, and if I had insight why not share what I knew as a rising expert?

"So many people began to admire how I did business, the hustle spirit I was starting to develop, and the grind I was on."

Make Them Stay: Build Your List

After years of hard work, I was starting to gain momentum. I was passionate about the message and word was spreading fast about what I was doing, and how. People were excited about it and wanted to support in whatever way they could. So what now? How do I keep it from being one encounter, and then allowing them to keep it moving, most likely to forget about the encounter eventually? The answer was simple; there has to be a way to retain your supporters, followers, and potential customers. Otherwise what is the point of building your brand? There is no point.

"The answer was simple; there has to be a way to retain your supporters, followers, and potential customers."

So exactly what is this concept and how does it work? Well many refer to it as building your list. In the past it has sometimes been referred to as growing your database. Whatever you want to call it, it's extremely important. If you have an online business, or even if you don't, the most standard way to build you list is through a subscription option. When people visit your website there is typically an option to subscribe and stay updated. Other forms of list building involve landing pages, or simply adding emails to your database manually. Figure out the best way to build and retain your following. Some even do it via social media groups.

"Figure out the best way to build and retain your following. Some even do it via social media groups."

Many businesses offer newsletters that you can subscribe to — some weekly, some monthly. In addition, times have changed and the ways to build your list have become a bit more creative. Another ideal way to build your list is with offers, usually free, that allow followers to opt in in order to receive the offer. From that point you can consider them added to your consumer library. My method was allowing people to create a profile for free on the website. Creating a profile would of course require entering your email address and other relative information, and just like that you were added to my database. What does this mean? I'm glad you asked.

"Another ideal way to build your list is with offers, usually free, that allow followers to opt in in order to receive the offer."

If you open a magazine and see an ad for a new clothing store, offering the same type of clothing that you wear, the same material, same quality, the same prices...and you need clothes for something, are you more prone to head over to your favorite store, or risk it by going to this new place even though it seems to be of the same caliber? The average person will go where they are familiar with the brand and believe in it. Lists allow you to reach your followers directly, and offer them what you need to — and a large percentage of the time they will buy. Even if they don't purchase all at once, if you continue to give value and engage your list, eventually something will be for them, and they will patronize.

"Lists allow you to reach your followers directly, and offer them what you need to — and a large percentage of the time they will buy."

The Follow Up-Bringing Home The Sale

If you're anything like me you hate harassing people. It's just not in my personality. My thought has always been that if you offer a good product or service and promote and market it effectively the right clients or customers will come. But it doesn't work that way. People work hard for their money, and they won't spend it easily. Especially if they don't feel like it's something they need. That's why it's so important to follow up. There are many ways to follow up without making it look like you're being a *buggaboo*. You can do the traditional follow up where you reach out to see if they have any questions or if they are still in need, letting them know how important working with you is. Or, you can reach back out to sweeten the deal. An example of this is sending an email to those who have showed interest in your product or service but haven't purchased yet letting them know that you are now offering 25% off of what they were interested in if they act now. Because who wouldn't want a sale?

"People work hard for their money, and they won't spend it easily."

Is It Working?-Measuring Your Progress

Where I was lacking was measuring progress, and there were a few ways this could be done. The first was via revenue...of course, I should be making money! What would I need to bring in revenue wise to make this worth my while and consider my hard work paying off? The other was website traffic. Although I knew HOW to drive traffic, I wasn't quite seeing the numbers. Third was personal measure. I had a certain person in mind to interview — and I said once I interviewed that person I could officially say I made it. Now that last one I left up to fate and hard work, but the other two I got to work on. My website host happens to have built in analytics. I started posting a certain way, and then recording the results. I immediately started to see an improvement in numbers.

"What would I need to bring in revenue wise to make this worth my while and consider my hard work paying off?"

Bottom line is you have to measure the progress in business. No way around it. How else will you know if you're succeeding? As mentioned, if you have a website one of the main things you want to measure is the amount of traffic. Traffic affects a lot of things; for one it affects the success of your business overall. The more people that know about your business, the more successful you're bound to become. Driving more traffic builds you a solid home on the internet, and will eventually reach people offline as well. Second, it increases revenue. Again, there are programs that will pay to advertise on your website; meaning the higher amount of visitors your site has, the more opportunity you have to make money. Clearly one of the most obvious ways to track your progress is to track your revenue. How are you selling?

"Driving more traffic builds you a solid home on the internet, and will eventually reach people offline as well."

Have you seen a rise in profit, or a drop? Clearly, if you have more customers than you did before you can assume that your business is making some sort of progress. Tracking progress serves so many purposes. If you have multiple products or services, it is important to track progress so that you can see what your best and least selling products are. This is important for things like fulfillment, orders etc. If you have vanilla cupcakes and truffle cupcakes and vanilla is your best seller, cutting back on the key ingredients for the truffle cupcakes and doubling on the vanilla may save a great deal of money.

"If you have multiple products or services, it is important to track progress so that you can see what your best and least selling products are."

There is software out there for analytics and of course there are good ole' surveys and polls in addition to reviews and audits on your business to see what's working and what's not; have you made progress or haven't you. There is no right or wrong way to measure your progress, just make sure you are clear on what's working, and that you're reaching your goals. Seeing improvement can also serve as motivation to keep going. There is nothing more satisfying than seeing numbers climb!

"There is no right or wrong way to measure your progress, just make sure you are clear on what's working, and that you're reaching your goals."

Who Said It Would Be Easy? Staying Motivated And Not Losing Hope

Running a business is one of the most difficult journeys you will embark upon — it is also the most rewarding if you remain dedicated and work smart. There will be times you may want to quit; times you wonder if it's worth it. Those are the times you must push through the most. Those are the times you take everything you've learned, and make it work. We now live in a digital age, which allows us to possibly share our products and services with people all over the country and even the world. Use it to your advantage. There are many resources out there, many teachers, many forms of inspiration — but if you ask any successful entrepreneur what made them successful a large percentage of them will say themselves. Embrace support along the way, but understand the success of your business is completely up to you.

"There will be times you may want to quit; times you wonder if it's worth it. Those are the times you must push through the most."

www.ingramcontent.com/pod-product-compliance
Lightning Source LLC
Chambersburg PA
CBHW081207180526
45170CB00006B/2245